Purse Cards

Large Purses

MATERIALS: 4$\frac{1}{4}$" x 8$\frac{1}{2}$" pattern paper • 4$\frac{1}{4}$" x 8$\frac{1}{2}$" solid paper • Button, charm, ribbon or pearls on a string • Wavy edge & straight edge scissors • Ruler • Adhesive

Small Purses

MATERIALS: 3" x 5" pattern paper • 3" x 5" solid paper • Gold cord • Wavy edge & straight edge scissors • Ruler • Adhesive

INSTRUCTIONS: Trim paper using the purse pattern. Glue pattern and solid papers together. Fold the bottom edge up creasing to make bottom edge of purse. Fold top down.

Glue button, ribbon or accessory to front of purse. Glue a strap of ribbon, pearls or other cord to the inside right and left edges of purse as a handle.

Fold

SMALL
PURSE
PATTERN

LARGE
PURSE
PATTERN

Card with Small Purse: Cut cardstock into a 4" x 4$\frac{1}{2}$" card. Decorate with additional paper layers as desired.

These little purses don't just hold a little money, credit cards, bank checks and coins... they hold good wishes and boundless love!

Tuck little purses into an envelope and write a cute message inside for a unique gift card.

Fold Design by Lani Temple

This shirt has also been independently designed by Gay Merrill Gross

Mother's Day

Shirts
MATERIALS: 3" x 3" printed papers • Wavy edge & straight edge scissors • Ruler • Adhesive
INSTRUCTIONS: Fold 3" x 3" papers following shirt instructions.

Skirts
MATERIALS: 2" x 6" printed papers • Scissors • Ruler • Adhesive
INSTRUCTIONS: Fold 2" x 6" papers following skirt instructions.
   Optional: Glue pleated skirt to a triangle base of white card stock to hold skirt to desired fullness. Glue shirt to top of skirt.

Bow or Scarf
MATERIALS: 1" x 8" printed papers • Scissors • Ruler • Adhesive
INSTRUCTIONS: Fold 1" x 8" papers following bow or scarf instructions. Glue bow or scarf under the collar of a shirt.

Cards: Cut cardstock into a 5½" x 8½" card. Fold card in half to 5½" x 4¼". Decorate with additional paper layers as desired.

Folded Shirt with Front Seam

1. Cut a 3" x 3" square of paper. Fold square in half, unfold.

2. Fold each half in half again to meet at center.

3. To find center, fold in half top to bottom, unfold.

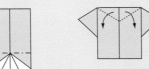

4. Fold bottom inside right and left corners out.

5. Fold bottom half back to meet top edge.

6. Fold top center right and left corners down to form collar.

7. Fold tip of shoulders back to round them off.

8. Optional: Fold sides diagonally to form taper.

9. Finished shirt.

Cuff Option: To make sleeve cuff and center button placket, make a small vertical fold along right and left edge of square paper before folding shirt.

Pleated Skirt

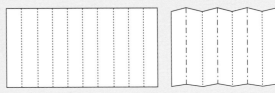

1. Cut a 2" x 6" strip of paper. To make pleats the same size and to fold accurately, lightly draw guidelines on the back of paper with a pencil and ruler.

2. Fold paper back and forth to crease along each line.

3. Shape accordion folds into a skirt. Stretch lower end to desired fullness and upper end to match width of bottom of shirt.

Folded Bow or Scarf

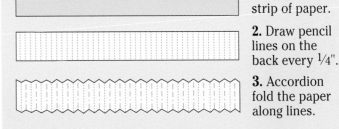

1. Cut a 1" x 8" strip of paper.

2. Draw pencil lines on the back every ¼".

3. Accordion fold the paper along lines.

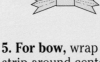

4. Cut a ¾" x 1" strip, fold long edges under ¼".

5. For bow, wrap strip around center of pleats. Glue, cut off excess. Spread out pleats at ends. Glue bow to dress.

6. For scarf, wrap strip around one end of pleats. Glue, cut off excess. Spread out pleats at ends. Glue bow to dress.

Mother's Day Cards... Mom will love a greeting made by hand just for her. Cute dresses, outfits and loads of love grace these unique cards.

Create clever cards and decorations by folding colorful shirts, skirts and bows. Make darling cards or simply hang them from a tiny clothesline with tiny clothespins.

Clever folded shirts, pants and skirts decorate elegant cards designed by Sheila Cunningham.

There is something here for everyone... clever cards for boys and girls of all ages! From team uniforms, elegant metallics and colorful papers to translucent Vellum.

Folded Shirt with No Seam

Fold Design by Rachel Katz

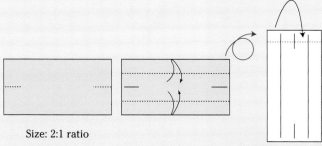

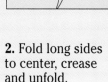

Size: 2:1 ratio

1. Cut a 3" x 6" rectangle of paper. With colored side up, pinch center of each short end.

2. Fold long sides to center, crease and unfold.

3. With white up, fold down top edge equal to side fold width.

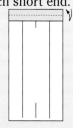

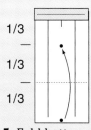

1/3

1/3

1/3

4. Fold the cut edge up to folded edge, crease and unfold.

5. Fold bottom edge up 1/3 the height of figure. Be accurate.

6. Unfold so top edge is cut edge again. Turn project over.

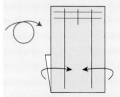

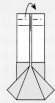

7. Fold long sides in to meet at center along existing creases.

8. Lift loose corners at bottom center and make slanted folds.

9. Fold top edge to back on top crease.

10. Fold top corners down to meet at intersection of horizontal crease and center line.

11. Lift bottom edge and slide it under points of collar. Crease at new bottom edge.

12. The completed shirt with opening at bottom where pant or skirt may be inserted.

Cuff Options: To form a white border on sleeves, fold a very narrow tapered hem on half of each long edge at Step 1. To form a white border on shirt bottom, fold up a small hem on a short edge at Step 1. If you want your shirt to be white with colored collar and hems, reverse all instructions.

Create a clever folded paper shirt then add a pleated skirt from translucent Vellum.

Shirts & Pants Cards

Shirts
MATERIALS: 3" x 6" printed papers • Scissors • Ruler • Adhesive
INSTRUCTIONS: Fold 3" x 6" papers following shirt instructions.

Pants
MATERIALS: 3" x 6" printed paper • Scissors • Ruler • Adhesive
INSTRUCTIONS: Fold 3" x 6" papers following pants instructions. See page 8. Glue shirt to top of pants.

Pleated Skirt
MATERIALS: 2" x 6" printed paper • Scissors • Ruler • Adhesive
INSTRUCTIONS: Fold 3" x 6" papers following skirt instructions. See page 4.

Optional: Glue pleated skirt to a triangle base of white card stock to hold skirt to desired fullness. Glue shirt to top of skirt.

Cards: Cut cardstock into a 5 1/2" x 8 1/2" card. Fold card in half to 5 1/2" x 4 1/4". Decorate with additional paper layers as desired.

Helpful Hint:
Try combining translucent printed Vellum, corrugated paper, pattern papers and metallic papers to create a beautiful hand-made look.

Create a darling hanging mobile with cute shirts, pants and skirts suspended from a paper 'hanger' with invisible thread.

Hanging Mobile

By Sheila Cunningham

Hanging Mobile

MATERIALS: Solid color card stock for the hanger • Assorted printed papers and/or translucent Vellum for clothes • 1/8" hole punch • Monofilament or 'invisible' thread • Wavy edge and straight edge scissors • Adhesive

INSTRUCTIONS: Assemble shirts, pants and skirt following instructions on pages 4, 7 and 9.

Punch a hole in each collar and tie 8" of monofilament through hole.

Cut 3 hangers from cardstock using pattern. Fold each hanger in half and glue together back to back catching the monofilament holding each outfit and a loop of monofilament at the top center between layers.

Hanger Pattern
for Mobile
- cut 3 -

Folded Pants

Fold Design by Rachel Katz

Size: 2:1 ratio

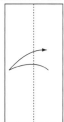 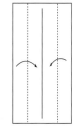 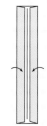

1. Cut a 3" x 6" rectangle of paper. With white side up, fold in half lengthwise. Crease and unfold.

2. Fold each half in half lengthwise to meet at center.

3. Fold in half again along existing crease.

4. Fold diagonally in half to make pants.

5. Slide pants into opening at bottom of shirt.

Hem option: To add a white hem, make a small fold along each short end of the rectangle as shown before starting. Then turn over before starting the folding diagram.

Helpful Hint:
For shirts, pants and skirts, choose printed papers that are white on one side. When folded, you will create a white collar and hems.

Tapered Skirt

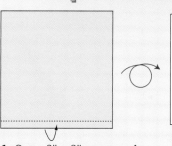 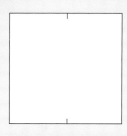

1. Cut a 3" x 3" square of paper. Fold up ¼" along one edge for hem band.

2. On reverse side mark center line.

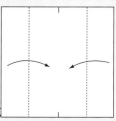

3. Fold sides in to center line.

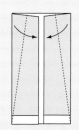 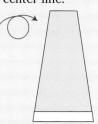

4. Tapering folds, bring upper outside corners to center.

5. Turn over and fit under shirt.

Card:
Cut cardstock into a 5½" x 8½" card. Fold card in half to 5½" x 4¼".
Decorate with additional paper layers and a small cord tie as desired.

Create the cutest cards ever...
from a clever clothesline with tiny
miniature clothespins to a 'Pajama Party' or
'Slumber Party' card with colorful folded P.J.s!

Specialty Cards

Shirts
MATERIALS: 3" x 3" printed papers • Scissors • Ruler • Adhesive
INSTRUCTIONS: Fold 3" x 3" papers following shirt instructions on page 4.

Pants
MATERIALS: 3" x 6" printed paper • Scissors • Ruler • Adhesive
INSTRUCTIONS: Fold 3" x 6" papers following pants instructions on page 9.

Shorts
MATERIALS: 3" x 3" printed paper • Scissors • Ruler • Adhesive
INSTRUCTIONS: Fold 3" x 3" papers following shorts instructions on page 11.

Cards: Cut cardstock into a 5½" x 8½" card. Fold card in half to 5½" x 4¼". Decorate with additional paper layers as desired.

Clothesline Card
MATERIALS: Use 8½" x 11" cardstock • a strip of die-cut green grass • two bamboo skewers • 9" of string • miniature clothespins • additional papers as desired.

Lady Bug Card
MATERIALS: Ladybug rubber stamp • Black and Red ink pads • White paper • 15" Red ribbon • cardstock • additional papers as desired.

'Pajama Party' Card
MATERIALS: Use 8½" x 11" cardstock • additional papers as desired.

Print or write "Pajama Party' or 'Slumber Party' information inside of the card.

Folded Shorts

1. Cut a 3" x 3" square of paper. Fold in half vertically, unfold.

2. Fold each half in half again to meet at center.

3. Fold in half toward back, across the width.

4. Finished shorts.

Cuff Option: On colored side, make a small horizontal fold along bottom edge of square paper before you start the folding diagram.

Helpful Hint:
Specialty greeting cards and calling cards can be expensive when purchased at boutique and stationery shops. With a little time and a minimum of money, it is easy to create memorable notes. Try making your own!

Calling Cards

Create unique little calling cards and envelopes to use as presents, package toppers, gift inserts or almost any occasion.

Shirts
MATERIALS: 3" x 3" pattern paper for shirts • 5" pieces of colored craft wire for hangers • Scissors • Ruler • Adhesive
INSTRUCTIONS: Fold shirt following instructions on page 4.

Cards: Cut cardstock into a 2¾" x 5" card. Fold card in half to 2¾" x 2½".

Envelopes: Cut translucent Vellum paper into a 3" x 3" square. Fold envelope following instructions on page 17.

Wire Clothes Hanger

1. Find center. Fold up ends ¾" from either side of center to make a triangle.

2. Twist both ends together about 3 times.

3. Using needle nose pliers, cut one end near twist.

4. Round other end and trim off extra wire with pliers.

Folded Tie

Helpful Hint:
*When learning to make a fold,
especially folds for detailed
items such as shirts and ties,
it often helps to practice
with a larger piece of paper.
Example: Use a 6" x 6" piece of practice
paper for a shirt, then use a 3" x 3"
piece of paper for the finished shirt.*

2.5 : 1.5 ratio

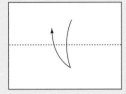 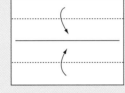

1. Cut a 2½" x 1½" piece of paper. Fold in half lengthwise, unfold.

2. Fold each half in half lengthwise to meet at center.

 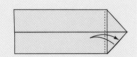

3. Fold top and bottom right corners to center.

4. Fold right point to left, unfold. Unfold top and bottom corners.

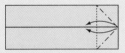 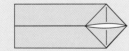

5. Pull inside center corners to center fold line.

6. Squeeze and push the fold open.

7. Fold left edge one third of way toward center.

8. Fold left fold in half toward front of tie.

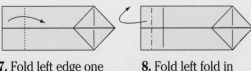

9. Fold long edges toward center forming angled sides.

10. Turn tie over.

Bow Tie

*Fold Design
by Lani Temple*

2:1 ratio

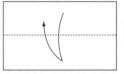 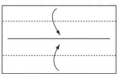 

1. Cut a 2" x 1" piece of paper. Fold in half lengthwise, unfold.

2. Fold each half in half lengthwise to meet at center.

3. Fold each corner toward center.

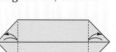 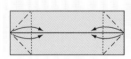 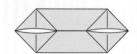

4. Fold right and left points in toward center. Unfold all corners.

5. Pull inside right and left corners toward center.

6. Squeeze and push the fold open.

Side profile

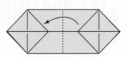 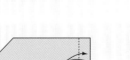 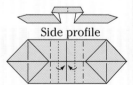

7. Fold in half right point to left point.

8. Fold center edge toward left and unfold. Unfold again.

9. Working with creases just made, fold each into center fold.

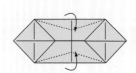 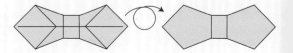

10. Fold top and bottom center folds towards middle.

11. Allow entire top and bottom sides to fold in at an angle.

12. Turn over.

HAPPY

FATHER'S DAY

Dad will love a card made with only him in mind. He can be comfortable by leaving his dress shirt in the closet... give him paper instead!

Helpful Hint:

Fold clever little shirts... a different color for each day of the week. Add a tiny folded tie and maybe a pocket and a button or two.

Father's Day

Shirts
MATERIALS: 3" x 3" printed papers (Shirt on card is 4" x 4") • Scissors • Ruler • Adhesive
INSTRUCTIONS: Fold 3" x 3" papers following shirt instructions on page 4.

Folded Ties
MATERIALS: 2½" x 1½" printed paper • Scissors • Ruler • Adhesive
INSTRUCTIONS: Fold 2½" x 1½" papers following tie instructions on page 12.

Bow Ties
MATERIALS: 2" x 1" printed paper • Scissors • Ruler • Adhesive
INSTRUCTIONS: Fold 2" x 1" papers following bow tie instructions on page 12.

Card: Cut cardstock into a 5½" x 8½" card. Fold card in half to 5½" x 4¼". Decorate with additional paper layers as desired.

Nothing is more special than a new baby! Welcome a child into the world with sweet cards featuring pink and blue shirts, diapers and accessories.

CONGRATULATIONS ON TWINS!

IT'S A GIRL

IT'S A BOY

Folded Diapers

Large Diaper
MATERIALS: 6" x 8" pattern paper • 6" x 8" cardstock or translucent Vellum paper • Pink or blue diaper pins • Wavy edge scissors • Ruler • Adhesive

INSTRUCTIONS: Cut 6" x 8" pattern paper using the large diaper pattern. Glue pattern to cardstock or Vellum paper.

Cut cardstock or Vellum ¼" larger than the pattern paper diaper.

Fold right top corner toward the center at an angle. Repeat on left side. Fold front of diaper up over the corners. Pin or glue diaper pins to front of diaper. Write a message inside the card.

Small Diaper
MATERIALS: 3" x 4" pattern paper • 3" x 4" cardstock or translucent Vellum paper • Small safety pins • Wavy edge scissors • Adhesive

INSTRUCTIONS: Cut 3" x 4" pattern paper using the large diaper pattern. Glue pattern to cardstock or Vellum paper.

Cut cardstock or Vellum ⅛" larger than the pattern paper diaper.

Fold right top corner toward the center at an angle. Repeat on left side. Fold front of diaper up over the corners. Pin diaper pins to front of diaper. Write a message inside the card.

Baby Cards

Shirts
MATERIALS: 3" x 3" printed papers (Shirt on card is 4" x 4") • Scissors • Ruler • Adhesive

INSTRUCTIONS: Fold 3" x 3" papers following shirt instructions on page 4.

Add a small wire hanger (page 11), a ribbon bow, punch paper hearts and/or baby buttons if desired.

Card: Cut cardstock into a 5½" x 8½" card. Fold card in half to 5½" x 4¼". Decorate with additional paper layers as desired.

SMALL DIAPER PATTERN

LARGE DIAPER PATTERN

Helpful Hint:
Combine several colors and patterns of 'blue' papers for a boy, or several colors and patterns of 'pink' for a girl.

Dainty Diapers for Your Darling

Lacy Shirt & Vest Cards

Vests

Large Vests: two 5½" x 8½" sheets of paper.
Small Vests: two 5" x 2½" sheets of paper.
MATERIALS: Two pattern papers, cardstock or Vellum • Buttons • Scissors • Ruler • Adhesive
INSTRUCTIONS: Cut and fold paper following vest instructions. Glue embellishments to front.

Folded Lacy Shirt
with Heart Button

**Cut two 4" x 8½" sheets of paper.
Place together back to back.**

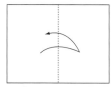

1. Find the center of paper.

2. Fold sides of 4" x 8½" paper to meet at center.

3. Fold top corners down to make collar.

4. Double fold collar back and underneath.

Optional Collar : Line the front with a paper doily to create a lacy collar when you fold the corners down.

Folded Vest

Large Vests: 5½" x 8½" sheet of paper.
Small Vests: 5" x 2½" sheet of paper.

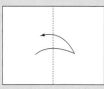

1. Fold rectangle in half, unfold.

2. Fold each side in half again, unfold.

3. Cut ½" to 1" slits at lower sides and center back.

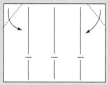 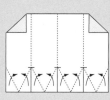

Optional Bottom: Fold the center only.

4. Fold top right corner down. Repeat on left.

5. Fold bottom corners to create a 'V' in the bottom of vest.

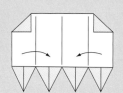 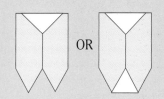

OR

6. Fold right and left sides in toward center fold line.

7. Finished vest.

aBEGINNER FOLDED PROJECT

Folded Envelope

1. Fold square diagonally in half both ways to find center, unfold.

2. Fold sides to center with edges overlapping about ³⁄₁₆".

3. Fold third corner up as shown and glue to secure.

Envelope of Hearts

MATERIALS: 5½" x 8½" White cardstock folded in half • 5½" x 4¼" Silver card stock • 5" x 3½" and 3" x 3" heart vellum • 3" x 4½" translucent Red vellum • Red vellum punched hearts • Wavy edge scissors • Adhesive

INSTRUCTIONS: Glue Silver card to White cardstock. Glue heart vellum to Silver card. Cut a wavy edge along all 4 sides of Red Vellum rectangle, glue to heart vellum.

Fold an envelope from 3" x 3" heart Vellum, glue along seams. Glue punched hearts to envelope.

Make truly unique wedding gift cards and invitations. Fold black and white translucent Vellum papers and cardstock into elegant 'Thank Yous' for friends and attendants and as a generous statement of your good wishes.

You're Invited

CONGRA